Eastern European Historical Repositories

Dr. Charles Dickson

HERITAGE BOOKS
2014

HERITAGE BOOKS
AN IMPRINT OF HERITAGE BOOKS, INC.

Books, CDs, and more—Worldwide

For our listing of thousands of titles see our website
at
www.HeritageBooks.com

Published 2014 by
HERITAGE BOOKS, INC.
Publishing Division
5810 Ruatan Street
Berwyn Heights, Md. 20740

Copyright © 2014 Dr. Charles Dickson

Heritage Books by the author:

Eastern European Historical Repositories

Religious Resources in American Libraries and Historical Associations

Scandinavian-American Genealogical Resources

International Standard Book Numbers
Paperbound: 978-0-7884-5582-7
Clothbound: 978-0-7884-6020-3

PREFACE

America has often been described as a melting pot nation. While such an adjective contains some truth it does not capture the total flavor of its multiethnic experience. While many national groups have blended into the American fabric, they have also, to varying degrees, maintained a sense of individual ethic identity.

This work represents an attempt to organize a list of the many resources that are available to serious students of Eastern European history in their ongoing search for family histories.

The term "resources" includes both national and local ethnic genealogical societies as well as institutional libraries of the various groups plus regional libraries in areas where large numbers of certain nationality groups have settled.

The author makes no claim that the lists are exhaustive, but this work is presented with the hope that it will inspire others to discover further resources.

In the final analysis, we will all become richer through expanding our knowledge of our roots.

Hickory, North Carolina 2014   C.D.

THE AUTHOR

Dr. Dickson is a college chemistry professor, ordained minister, and student of genealogy. He holds degrees from the University of Tampa, Wartburg Theological Seminary, Stetson University and the University of Florida.

He has authored books in chemistry and religion, plus a previous one in genealogy titled, *Scandinavian Historical Resources.* His genealogical articles have appeared in Heritage Quest, Ancestry Newsletter, the Polish-American Newsletter, Genealogical Helper, the American Dane, and the Finnish-American Newsletter.

He is a Swedish American whose grandparents came to Jamestown, New York in the 1870s. His boyhood was spent in Youngstown, Ohio, a town rich in Eastern European traditions. This book is the result of his lifelong interest in American ethnic history.

TABLE OF CONTENTS

Preface   iii
The Author   iv
Table of Illustrations   vi
Introduction   vii
Albanians   1
Armenians   6
Bulgarians   14
Croatians   20
Czechs
(including Bohemians and Moravians)   27
Estonians   36
Greeks (including Cypriots)   41
Hungarians (including Magyars)   49
Latvians   54
Lithuanians   60
Poles (including Pomeranians and Silesians) 66
Romanians (including Moldavians)   74
Russians (including Byelorussians)   85
Serbians
(including Bosnians and Macedonians)   95
Slovaks (including Carpatho-Rusyns)   101
Slovenians   109
Ukrainians (including Ruthenians)   117
General Bibliography   125

TABLE OF ILLUSTRATIONS

Letterhead of Albanian Orthodox Archdiocese	3
Armenian Cultural Foundation	9
Bulgarian newspaper head	15
Croatian Fraternal Union	23
Czech and Slovak Museum	29
Moravian Archives letterhead	33
Estonian church periodical	37
Logo of Greek Orthodox Archdiocese	44
Magyar marketing advertisement	50
Letterhead of American Hungarian Society	51
Latvian church periodical	55
Logo of Latvian church	56
Books on Latvian immigration	57
Lithuanian Research Studies Center	62
Polish Costume Display	67
Holy Mother of the Rosary Cathedral	68
Savonarola Theological Seminary	69
Logo of the Kashubian Association	71
Logo of the Romanian Cultural Center	76
Romanian Ethnic Art Museum	77
Traditional pottery, Romanian Ethnic Art Museum	78
St. Mary's Romanian Orthodox Church	81
St. Michael's Russian Orthodox Church	86
Logo of St. Vladimir's Theological Seminary	88
Logo of Holy Trinity Orthodox Seminary	89
St. Tikhon's Theological Seminary	90
St. Herman's Theological Seminary	91
Logo of the IHRC	97
Slovak Museum	104
Historic St. Josephs Slovenian Church	110
Slovenian Settlements Map	112
Slovenian Library	114
Logo of the Ukrainian National Association	119
Ukrainian History publications	120
Dome of SS Cyril and Methodius Seminary church	121

INTRODUCTION TO
EASTERN EUROPEAN RESOURCES

In contrast to those who migrated from Northern Europe and the British Isles, immigrants to America from Eastern Europe did not begin arriving in significant numbers until the mid to late 19th century. Entering a nation in which the Irish had already become well-established in Massachusetts, as were the Germans in Pennsylvania, the Scandinavians in the upper Midwest, the French in Maine and Louisiana, and the English in many areas, these natives of Eastern European lands found themselves at distinct language, cultural ,and economic disadvantages.

In spite of all this, they were able to band together in dozens of support groups, religious institutions, and ethnic associations which not only assisted them to survive physically, emotionally, and spiritually, but also became valuable repositories for historical information relating to each group.

The listings in this book cover the following ethnic groups: Albanians, Armenians, Bulgarians, Croatians, Czechs, Estonians, Greeks, Hungarians, Latvians, Lithuanians, Poles, Romanians, Russians, Serbians, Slovaks, Slovenians, and Ukrainians.

Under each ethnic group a common format has been followed which includes an introduction to immigration patterns, followed by separate page listings describing the holdings of primary genealogical societies, museums, and educational institutions associated with that group. Next there are listings of other ethnic related societies which have some family histories followed by a listing of the regional public libraries located in areas where each particular group has settled in significant numbers.

As the reader uses this handbook as a research tool in discovering group and family histories, hopefully he or she will be reminded that the American multiethnic experience may be singularly unique in human history.

One is reminded of Walt Whitman's observation in his preface to the 1855 edition of *Leaves Of Grass*: "Here in these States at last is something in the doings of man that corresponds with the broadcast doings of day and night. Here is not merely a nation, but a teeming nation of nations."

ALBANIANS

Settlers from Albania came in small numbers to the United States prior to World War I, but exact numbers are difficult to ascertain since many were listed by immigration officials as being Turks. Some estimates say there were as many as 80,000 by the 1940s but about half returned to their home-land.

The first permanent settlers came to the Boston area and from there to other parts of Massachusetts. There were also Albanian communities in Manchester and Concord, New Hampshire as well as Pawtucket, Rhode Island and in some of Maine's shoe and textile towns. Bridgeport, Hartford, and Waterbury, Connecticut also received groups of Albania immigrants, while others scattered to locations in Michigan, Wisconsin, Ohio, Illinois, Indiana, Minnesota, Utah, Pennsylvania, Missouri, Washington, California, and northern New York.

Boston remains the center of the largest Alabanian-American concentration followed by Jamestown, New York. The bulk of Albanian immigrants are Eastern Orthodox Christians with a significant minority belonging to the Moslem faith and a small number holding membership in various Protestant denominations. The major Orthodox bodies are the Albanian Orthodox Archdiocese who presiding bishop and headquarters are located in Boston and the Albanian Orthodox Diocese which is headquartered in Jamaica Plain, Massachusetts. The first group consists of thirteen congregations and the latter having seven.

Moslem Albanians are concentrated for the most part in Peabody and New Bedford, Massachusetts and in St. Louis, Missouri. There are Roman Catholic Albanian parishes in New York and Chicago.

The Albanian Orthodox churches train men for the priesthood at St. Vladimir's Orthodox Theological

Seminary, located in Yonkers, New York and they are also aligned in the Orthodox Church in America.

THE ALBANIAN ORTHODOX ARCHDIOCESE OF AMERICA 529 East Broadway, South Boston, Massachusetts 02127. This is the national headquarters for a church composed primarily of Albanian immigrants and their descendants. The entire Archdiocese consists of about 20 parishes having approximately 40,000 members.

Albanian Orthodox parishes are located in the cities of Boston, Natick, Southbridge, and Worcester in the state of Massachusetts; in Jamestown, Rochester, and New York City New York; as well as Bridgeport, Connecticut; Detroit, Michigan; Cleveland, Ohio; and Philadelphia, Pennsylvania.

While individual parishes maintain family and parish records of their immediate areas, the Archdiocesan headquarters has valuable historical records dating back to 1918 and the beginning of Albanian Church work which was, in the early days, under the guidance of the Russian Orthodox Church.

Parishes of
The Albanian Orthodox Archdiocese

Letterhead of the Archdiocese

3

Additional Albanian Resources

Albanian Research List, 144 Marine St., St. Augustine, FL 32084

Albanian America Catholic League, 4221 Park Ave., Bronx, NY 10457

Albanian Orthodox Church, 54 Burroughs, Jamaica Plain, MA 02130

Albanian Orthodox Archdiocese, 529 Broadway, S. Boston, MA 02127

Boston Public Library, 666 Boylston, Boston, MA 02117

Bridgeport Public Library, 925 Broad St., Bridgeport, CT 06604

Concord Public Library, 45 Green St., Concord, NH 03301

Fenton Historical Society, Washington St., Jamestown, NY 14701

James Prendergast Library, 508 Cherry St., Jamestown, NY 14701

Manchester Historical Association Library, 129 Amherst St., Manchester, NH 03101

Massachusetts State Historical Soceity, 1194 Boylston, Boston, MA 02215

Mattatuck Historical Society Library, W. Main St. Waterbury, CT 06702

Pawtucket Public Library, 13 Summer St., Pawtucket, RI 02860

Albanian Bibliography

Burgess, T.A. Report on the Albanians Springfield 1913

Chekrezi, Constantine. Albania; Past and Present Arno 1975

Federal Writers Project The Albanian Struggle AMS 1973

Nagi, Dennis The Albanian-American Odyssey AMS 1988

Pollo, Stafannaq History of Albania Routledge 1980

Vickers, Miranda Albania: A Modern History St. Martins 1994

ARMENIANS

In 1655 two Armenian immigrants came to America, brought by the governor of colonial Virginia for the purpose of nurturing silk worms. Since that time Armenians in America have engaged in many arts and crafts industries and some have achieved international reputations in these fields. In addition there are prosperous farmers of Armenian extraction who are instrumental in grape ·and wine production in California.

Migration of Armenians began in the early 1900s but has never been as heavy as many other ethnic groups. There are an estimated 150,000 Americans of Armenian extraction.

Proportionately the state of California has the largest number centered around Fresno, Los Angeles, and San Francisco. Their geographic distribution in the United States is indicated by the eleven cities having the largest number of Armenians: Fresno, California, New York City, Detroit, Boston, Providence, Philadelphia, Union City, N.J., Los Angeles, Waterton, and Worcester, Massachusetts, and Chicago.

The majority of Armenians belong to the Gregorian or Armenian Apostolic Church, but there are also Armenian Protestant (mainly Presbyterian) and some Armenian Catholic churches under the Armenian Catholic Exarchate. The Gregorian or Armenian Apostoic Churches are divided ·into the Armenian Apostoic Church of America with 40 parishes scattered throughout the United States and Canada and the Armenian Church of North and South America divined into an eastern diocese with thirty-five congregations and a western diocese with eighteen. The St Nersess Armenian Seminary of New Rochelle, New York trains priests.

The Armenian Catholic Exarchate is headquartered in Wynnewood, Pennsylvania and has five parishes which support four schools and four religious communities.

As a result of later immigration, Armenian families tend to be bilingual, preserving the language and customs of the homeland.

ARMENIAN LIBRARY AND MUSEUM OF AMERICA
65 Main Street, Watertown; Massachusetts 02172.This is a
very rich repository of Armenian cultural, family, and
religious history

The library contains more than 12,000 volumes which are
available to the researcher of family histories. There·are also
special collections including one of early printings dating
from 1514 - 1700 plus oral histories and audio and visual
tapes. Of special interest is a replica of a 13th century
Armenian church known as the Katoghike which stood in
the Armenian capital city of Yerevan.

Opportunities abound for research and discovery at this
well-maintained facility in the heart of Armenian
settlements in New England.

ARMENIAN CULTURAL FOUNDATION 441 Mystic·Street Arlington, Massachusetts 02174. This museum is housed in a beautiful old restored mansion and has more .than 10,000 volumes relating to Armenia and Armenian-American cultural history under the direction of curator, Hagop Atamian. In addition to family histories relating to the American experience there is also a sizeable collection of materials on Armenian art and literature.

This great collection reminds one of the one of the observation of Professor Lehmann Haupt, in his book, *Armenia: Past and Present*, in which he wrote, "The more we fathom their distant past, the more we begin to realize the constructive and enlightening role played by the Armenians in the world history of civilization."

ST. NERSESS ARMENIAN SEMINARY 150 Stratton Road New Rochelle, New York 10804. The seminary was established in 1961 under the dioceses of the Armenian Church. The Archbishop Tiran Nersoyan Memorial Library is named after the founder of the seminary. Its purpose is to prepare priests for service in the Armenian Church.

Though relatively small the library has some very diverse holdings devoting care ·and attention to classical Armenian books. The Krikor and Clara Zohrab Information center in association with St. Nersess is also an excellent source of family and parish records for early Armenian immigrants and churches in America.

Armenian Assembly of America, 1140 19th St. NW - Suite 600, Washington, DC 20036
Ph (202) 393-3434 Fax (202) 638-/904
www.aaa inc.org

National Association for Armenian Studies 395 Concord Avenue, Belmont, MA 02476
Ph (617) 489-1610 Fax (617) 484-1759
www.naas-r.org

Society for Armenian Studies California State University, 5245 N. Racker Ave PB4, Fresno, CA 93740-8001
Ph. (559) 278-2669
www.barlow@csu.fresno.edu

Additional Armenian Resources

Arlington Historical Society, 7 Jason St. Arlington, MA 02174

Armenian Educational Council, 1130 Mass Ave NW, Washington, DC 20005

Armenian Church of America, 630 2nd Ave., New York, NY 10016

Boston Public Library, 666 Boylston, Boston, MA, 02117
Chicago Public Library, 425 N. Michigan, Chicago, IL 60606

Fresno Free·Library, 2420 Mariposa St., Fresno, CA 93721

National Association for Armenian Studies and ·Research, 6 Divinty Avenue, Cambridge,·MA 02138

New York Public Library, 5th & 42nd New York, NY 100l8

Mekhitarist Fathers, 1327 Pleasant Ave. Los Angeles, CA·90033

Mekhitarist Fathers,·100 Mt. Auburn, Cambridge, MA 02138

Saddle Brook Public Library, 340 Hayhill, Saddle Brook, NJ 07162

University of Michigan-Dearborn Armenian Research Center, 4901 Evergreen Road, Dearborn, MI 48128

Western Diocese-Armenian Church, S. Crenshaw, Los Angeles, CA 90005

Worcester Public Library, Salem Square, Worcester, MA 01608

Armenian Bibliography

Agasayan, Larisa An Armenian Immigrant in America, Bookshelf 1994

Avakian, Arra The Armenians in America, Lerner 1977

Derounian, A. History of Armenians in California, Lippincott. 1946

Jafferian, Serpoohi Winds of Destiny, National Assn. 1993

Mahakian, C. History of Armenians in California, Oceana 1978

Malcolm, M.V. The Armenians in America, Pilgrim 1912

Vassilian, V. Armenian Yellow Pages, Armenians Ref. Bks. 1993

Wertsmann, Valdimir The Armenians in America, Oceana 1978

BULGARIANS

Bulgaria is a republic of Europe situated in the Balkan Peninsula with a population of eight million. The language belongs to the southern group of Slavic languages and employs the Cyrillic alphabet in writing.

Bulgarian immigration to the United States dates back to second half of the 19th century. It is somewhat difficult to determine the exact numbers of immigrants who came in those early days since many were listed as being Turks, which controlled part of Bulgaria. Also those who were Moslem in religion tended to be listed as Turks while those who were Eastern Orthodox Christians were sometimes listed as Greeks or Yugoslavians for record purposes.

Americans of Bulgarian ancestry are scattered throughout the nation but tend to concentrate in cities of more than 100,000 population and usually marked by heavy industry including the states of Michigan, Pennsylvania, Ohio, Indiana, New York, and Illinois. Cities with highest Bulgarian populations include Detroit, Chicago, Gary and Ft. Wayne, Indiana, Rochester, New York, and the Ohio cities of Toledo, Akron, Cleveland, Columbus, and Youngstown.

Most Bulgarians are affiliated with the Bulgarian Orthodox Church which has fifteen parishes in these states with a metropolutan residing at the Cathedral of St. Andrey in New York.

The first Bulgarian Orthodox Church, Sts. Cyrillius and Methodius, was organized in Granite City , Illinois in 1909.

A few Protestant churches (Methodist, Presbyterian and Baptist) were organized in various parts of Illinois including Chicago as well as in St. Louis and Detroit.

It has been estimated there are about 75,000 Americans of Bulgarian ancestry. A Bulgarian Orthodox School is maintained in Steelton, Pennsylvania.

Symbol on the front of a Bulgarian newspaper
published in America

BULGARIAN EASTERN ORTHODOX CHURCH 550-A West 50th Street, New York, New York 10019. This church, organized as a diocese headed by a Metropolitan who resides at a Cathedral in New York City, is composed of about 80,000 members in thirteen parishes. They are located primarily in urban industrial areas including Akron, Cincinnati, Cleveland, and Lorain, Ohio; Buffalo, New York; Detroit, Michigan; and Indianapolis, Indiana; as well as Los Angeles, California; and West Palm Beach, Florida.

Many parish and family records are maintained in local parishes and the diocesan headquarters and Cathedral in New York has much valuable information relating to Bulgarian immigration to the United States.

FEEFHS, P. O. Box 510898, Salt Lake City, Utah 84151-0898. WWW: http://feefths.org. This is an international organization of genealogical research scholars which focuses on Eastern Europe including Bulgarian, Serbian, Russian, Polish, Slovak, Slovenian, Romanian, and Ukrainian migration. They are engaged in researching family records in both the United States and Eastern Europe. This work includes microfilming and cataloging of parish and community records, publishing a quarterly journal and disseminating genealogical information to those interested in learning more about their Eastern European roots.

Additional Bulgarian Resources

Akron-Summit County Library, 55 S. Main, Akron, Ohio 44326

Allen County Public Library, 900 Webster, Ft. Wayne, IN 46801

Bulgarian Orthodox Church, 312 W. 101 St, New York, NY 10025

Chicago Public Library, 125 N. Michigan, Chicago, IL 60606

Cleveland Public Library 325 Superior, Cleveland, OH 44103

Columbus Metropolitan Library, 96 S. Grant, Columbus, OH 43215

Detroit Public Library, 5201 Woodward, Detroit, MI 48202

Gary Public Library, 220 W. 5th St., Gary, IN 46402

New York Public Library, 5th & 42nd New York, NY 10018

Public Library-Youngstown, 350 Wick, Youngstown, OH 44503

Rochester History Society, 485 East Ave. Rochester, NY 14607

Bulgarian Bibliography

Altanikov, Nickolay The Bulgarian Americans, Ragasan 1979

Arastasoff, Christ The Tragic Peninsula, Blackwell 1938

Anastasoff, Christ The Bulgarians, Universe Books 1977

Kolar, Walter Cultural History of Bulgaria Tamburitza 1981

Legio, George Bulgaria: Past and Present, Ams Press 1973

Roucek, Hoseph Politics of the Balkans, McGraw-Hill 1939

CROATIANS

Croatia is one of the republics of the former Yugoslavian nation which has recently emerged as an independent nation. It has about five million people most of whom speak the Serbo-Croatian language. The Droatians use Roam characters in writing their language as opposed to the Serbians who employ the Cyrillic alphabet.

Historical records indicate that some Croatians were among the Yugoslavian sailors who came to the port of New Orleans in the 18th century. But it wasn't until the middle of the 19th century that they began to settle in significant numbers. While some Croatians remained in New Orleans some others would later be drawn into the gold rush to California in the mid-19th century. In addition some found employment in the Savannah, Georgia area where they worked in the silk industry.

Most Croatians are members of the Roman Catholic Church, belonging to parishes scattered throughout the United States. Cleveland, Ohio has the largest Croatian population of any American city and remains a center for Croatian cultural and religious organizations. St. Paul's Church is located there and maintains a school which is operated by the Franciscan Sisters. In nearby Youngstown, the Saints Peter and Paul Church is also Croatian as is the St. Jerome Church in Detroit. New York City, Pittsburgh, and Chicago also have significant Croatian populations.

There are also Croatian communities scattered in various parts of the south, particularly in Texas.

There are about 500,000 Americans of Croatian ancestry.

CROATIAN ETHNIC INSTITUTE 4851 S. Drexel Boulevard, Chicago, Illinois 60615. The institute was founded in 1975 by the Croatian Franciscans and has, since that time, developed an archives with a large repository of personal papers, manuscripts and correspondence of many Croatian-Americans.

The library contains over 12,000 volumes plus collections of parish records, census, and annual reports. There are also documents and records of cultural, fraternal, political organizations, sports clubs, musical societies, travel agencies, and businesses. The museum also holds artistic and historical items related to the Croatian heritage, and is an excellent resource agency.

RAGUSAN PRESS - Croatian Immigration Center - 2527 San Carlos Avenue, San Carlos, California 94070.
Tel 650-592-1190
www.croatian.com

Ragusan Press is a primary source for information regarding Croatian immigration to the United States. Formerly called the Croatian-Slovenian-Serbian Genealogical Society it has a library of more than 10,000 volumes. It continues to focus on these three immigrant groups, not only by maintaining family and historical records, but also assists in the dissemination of information through vigorous publishing efforts.

THE CROATIAN FRATERNAL UNION 3441 Forbes Ave. Pittsburgh, Pennsylvania 15225. This institution represents 105 years of Croatian-American history and has more than 86,000 members scattered in communities throughout America.

In addition to publishing a periodical titled ZAJEDNICAR, it contains family and parish records of Croatian-American communities in Detroit, Gary, Indiana, Chicago, Cleveland

The Croatian Fraternal Union Headquarters

and Youngstown in Ohio as well as Johnstown, Farrell, and Pittsburgh, Pennsylvania and some smaller communities such as Calumet in the upper peninsula of Michigan.

Additional Croatian Resources

Association for Croatian Studies, John Carrol U., Cleveland, OH 44118

Carnegie Library, 41100 Forbes, Pittsburgh, PA 15213

Cleveland Public Library, 325 Superior, Cleveland, OH 44103

Croatian Genealogy Home Page, PO Box 4327, Davis, CA 95617

Croatian Information Serv. PO Box 660546, Arcadia, CA 91006

Croatian National Association, 1608 Fremont, Alhambra, CA 91803

Croatian National Congress, 10 Ackerman Dr., Saddel River, NJ 071158

Public Library-Youngstown 350 Wick, Youngstown, OH 44503

Croatian Bibliography

Bennett, Linda Croats and Slovences in Washington, DC, Ragusan 1978

Eterevich, Adam Croatian Pioneers in America, Ragusan 1979

Kraljic, F. Croatian Migration, Raguean 1988

Mihanovich, C. S. Americanization of the Croats, Ragusan 1971

Omeranin, Ivo Anglo-American Croatian Repproachment, Ivor 1989

Prpic, George The Croatian Immigrants in America, Ragusan 1971

Shapiro, Ellen 'I'he Croatian American, Chelsea 1989

CZECHS

The Czech Republic comprises the western two-thirds of the former Czechoslovakia and has about eleven million people. They also include the categories of Bohemians and Moravians. Czech Moravians came to the United States in the early 1700s and established the towns of Bethlehem, Pennsylvania and Salem (now Winston-Salem), North Carolina. German Moravians also composed a considerable part of both groups.

But the bulk of Czech immigrants came in two waves during the 19th century. The first Czechs settled in Chicago while those from Bohemia and western Moravia settled chiefly in the northern states and those from northeastern Bohema and eastern Moravia went to Texas. Towns such as Moravia, Texas and New Prague, Minnesota were founded by these immigrants. In the 1940s Czech Americans constituted ¼ of the population of Cedar Rapids, Iowa, 1/7 of Cleveland, and 1/8 of both Gary, Indiana and Omaha, Nebraska.

While significant numbers of Czechs joined Moravian, Presbyterian and other Protestant groups about half of all Czech immigrants maintained membership in the Roman Catholic Church. They support St. Procopius College at Lisle, Illinois, the only Czech college in America, and three academies, one in Chicago, one in Omaha, and one in Shiner Texas.

Czech and German Moravians of the Moravian Province in the northern United States established the Moravian College and Theological Seminary for the training of clergy for that church. The Southern Province of the Moravian Church supports Salem College in Winston-Salem, North Carolina.

There is also a smaller group of Moravians known as the Czech Moravian Brethren in America whose congregations are located primarily in Texas.

There are about 400,000 American of Czech descent.

THE NATIONAL, CZECH AND SLOVAK MUSEUM AND LIBRARY 30 16th Avenue SW, Cedar Rapids, Iowa 52404. The museum and library was established in 1973 for the purpose of preserving Czech and Slovak heritage. It is a rich treasury of historical records dating back to early immigration in eastern Iowa (the 1850s) when the first parish churches were established.

The Czech and Slovak Museum and Library

In addition to parish and family records there is a sizeable collection arts works, printing presses, musical instruments and numerous other objects of historical interest.

SLAVIC RESEARCH INSTITUTE 31910 Road 160 Visalia, California 93292. The institute specializes in working with researchers whose family roots are in Bohemia and Moravia and has 500 historical and genealogical books on immigration from these areas. It also provides searches of regional records dating back to the 1600s. These include baptismal, marriage, and death records as well as computerized family history books and listings of family names and occupations.

WILBER CZECH MUSEUM 102 West 3rd Street Wilber, Nebraska 68465. Czech immigration to various Nebraska towns in the late 19th century reached significant proportions especially in the larger town such as Omaha. Czechs in the small town of Wilbcr, Nebraska have preserved their cultural and family histories in the Wilber Czech Museum organized 30 years ago. At the center of the museum is the Dvoracek Memorial Library which houses 12,000 volumes of local Czech family histories.

Also in the museum ia a Czech Heritage Center which features rare books from Czechoslovakia plus antique dolls, paintings and costumes. Another unique feature is a section containing replicas of early immigrant homes and businesses. The museum also has published several books on local Czech family history.

ILLINOIS BENEDICTINE COLLEGE - Theodore Lownik Library 5700 College Road, Lisle, Illinois 60532-0900. The college was founded in 1887 by Czech Catholics of the Benedictine Order. The library has 124,000 volumes including some valuable historical material relating to the Benedictine Order plus Czech Catholic family and parish histories in the·midwest.

THE MORAVIAN ARCHIVES 41 West Locust Street, Bethlehem, Pennsylvania 18018-2757. The Archives compose the historical records of the northern province of the Moravian Church. The church is so-named since it originated in the 15th century with the Protestant Reformation in the area of the current Czech Republic known as Moravia.

Members of the Moravian Church who came to America founded the towns of Bethlehem, Pennsylvania and Salem (now Winston-Salem) North Carolina. They were both of German and Czech nationalities. The Archives constitutes a rich source for those wishing to do genealogical research. There are several million pages of manuscripts in many languages plus more than 30,000 published items and a collection of rare books and manuscripts relating to early Moravian families and churches.

THE MORAVIAN ARCHIVES

41 West Locust Street, Bethlehem, Pennsylvania 18018-2757
Telephone: (610) 866-3255   FAX: (610) 866-9210

Letterhead of the Moravian Archives

Additional Czech Resources

Cedar Rapids Public Library, 500 1st SE Cedar Rapids, Iowa 52401

Czech Cultural Club, 2254 S. 13th St Omaha, Nebraska 68103

Czech-Moravian-Bohemian   Geneal.   Page
http://iarelatve.com/czech

Forsyth County Library, 660 W 5th St. Winston-Salem, N. C. 27101

Gnaddenhutten Public Library, 160 Walnut, Gnaddenhutten, Ohio 44629

Moravian College, Reeves Library, Bethlehem, Pennsylvania 18018

Moravian Archives, 41 Locust St. Bethlehem, Pennsylvania 18018

Omaha Public Library, 215 S. 15th St. Omaha, Nebraska 68102

Salem College Library, Salem Square, Winston-Salem, N.C. 27108

Moravian Church Archives, 4 E. Bank St., Winston-Salem, N.C. 27101

Unity of the Brethren, 2205 Carnation, Temple, Texas 76501

Czechoslovak General Society, Box 16225, St. Paul, MN 55116

International Association of Teachers of Czech, P.O. Box 7217, Austin, Texas 78713

Czech Bibliography

Bieha, Karel The Czechs in Oklahoma, U of Okla, Pr. 1980

Capek, Thomas The Czechs in America, Greenwood 1974

Hudson, E. Czech Pioneers in the Southwest, S. W. Press 1934

Kutak, Robert Story of a Bohemian-American Village, Ayer 1970

Laska, Vera The Czechs in America, Oceana 1978

Roucek, Joseph Czechs and Slovaks in America, Lerner 1967

Sakson-Ford S. Czech Americans, Chelsea 1989

ESTONIANS

Estonia is the northernmost nation of the three Baltic republics which were once part of the former Soviet Union but have now achieved independence. This nation of about two million people speaks a language which is part of the Finno-Ugric division of the Ural Altaic family of languages and is related to Finnish and Hungarian.

There is very little information about Estonian immigrants prior to World War I since many of them carried Russian pass-ports and were therefore listed as Russians.

While there were some early settlements in the Dakotas prior to World War I the majority of immigrants came after the 1920s to seaport towns such as New York and San Fransciso although some settled on farms near Irma and Gleason, Wisconsin and another sizeable group came to Tacoma and Spokane, Washington. Some 2,000 would also settle in Massachusetts, Connecticut, and Rhode Island plus smaller groups in Vermont, New Hampshire, Pennsylvania, and Virginia.

About 80·percent of Estonians are Lutherans and most of the remainder are members of the Eastern Orthodox communion. An Estonian Lutheran Synod has been organized in the United States with an archbishop whose headquarters are located in Toronto, Ontario. Numerous congregations of the Evangelical Lutheran Church in America, particularly in New York City, Chicago, Minneapolis, Milwaukee, and Seattle provide church services in the Estonian language.

There is also an Estonian Eastern Orthodox Church whose bishop and headquarters are in Los Angeles.

There are an estimated 60,000 Estonians living in the United States.

Usu ☧ Sõna

I. .... Veebruar, 1953 Nr. 2

Sa ule Jumal valvaku.

Mu armas isamaa.

Ta olgu sinu kaitseja

Ja võlku rohkesť õunisia,
Mis iial ette põtaõ sa,
Mu kallis isamaa.

*Front cover of an Estonian American church periodical
published in the 1950s*

ESTONIAN HISTORICAL ARCHIVES 607 East 7th Street, Lakewood, New Jersey 08701. These archives were developed from the efforts of the Estonian Relief Committee which has endeavored to help Estonians settle in the United States.

The library contains some 4,000 books plus oral histories and ship records.

There are particularly detailed family records as immigrants sponsored by the Committee were required to supply extensive biographical data which also included their occupations.

Additional Estonian Resources

Boston Public Library, 666 Boylston, Boston, Massachusetts 02117

Enoch Pratt Public Library, Cathedral St. Baltimore, Md. 21201

Estonian Ev. Lutheran Church, Sunrise Ave. Toronto, Ontario, M4A 2R1

Estonian Orthodox Church, Fountain Ave., Los Angeles, California 90019

Free Library of Philadelphia, 1901 Vine St., Philadelphia, PA 19103

New York Public Library, 5th & 42nd, New York, New York 10018

San Francisco Public Library, Civic Center, San Francisco, CA 94115

Tacoma Public Library, 1102 Tacoma Ave., Tacoma, WA 98401

Seattle Geneal. Society Library, 8511 15th Ave NE, Seattle, ·WA 98111

Estonian Bibliography

Jackson, John Estonia, Greenwood 197'l

Halajaspold, J. Estonians in America, Baltic Times 1939

Pullerits, Albert Estonia, AMS 1977

Roucek, Joseph The American Estonians, Baltic Times 1936

Walko, M. A. Maintaining Estonian Ethnicity, AHS 1988

GREEKS

The story of Greek America began in 1768 when a Scottish physician, Dr. Andrew Turnbull, brought his Greek wife to an area of the east coast of Florida, now known as New Smyrna. The colony lasted about 10 years when the few who stayed in America moved to nearby St. Augustine.

But the majority of Greek immigration to America came between the years of 1901 and 1930 when an estimated 460,000 arrived, a figure representing nearly 10 percent of the total population of Greece. The new immigrants tended to engage in commercial and shipping occupations, rather than in rural types jobs such as farming. The Greek community is known worldwide for their skills in the restaurant business.

Patterns of immigration show the tendency of Greeks to settle in urban areas. While distribution of such settlements is widespread, it is primarily in the large cities of each state where we find concentrations of Greek settlers. New York has the largest concentration of Greek Americans followed by Illinois, Massachusetts, California, Pennsylvania, and Ohio. In two smaller towns; Tarpon Springs, Florida and Lowell, Massachusetts, Greek Americans represent the major ethnic group. Other major cities with large Greek populations include New York, Chicago, Detroit, San Francisco, Boston, Los Angeles, Philadelphia, Washington, Pittsburgh, St. Louis, Cleveland, and Milwaukee.

The vast majority of Greeks are of the Eastern Orthodox faith. There are more than 600 parishes under the jurisdiction of the Greek Archdiocese of North and South America. Hellenic College and Holy Cross Theological Seminary for the training of priests are maintained in Brookline, Massachusetts. A small percentage of Greeks are Roman Catholic and are part of the various jurisdictions in which they reside. There are an estimated 3 million Americans of Greek ancestry.

GREEK FAMILY HERITAGE COMMITTEE 100 Main Street, Huntington, New York 117113-6990. Rather than a single museum or archival collection, this program under the direction of Antonia Mattheou, represents an extensive reference on more than twenty Greek historical associations and archival collections in the New York area. All of these have early family and immigration records including such groups as the Greek Cultural Center, the Greek American Folklore Society, The American Institute for Dodecanesian Studies, the Benevolent Cyprian Society, and many parish records of Greek Orthodox Churches in the there. There is more than 800 linear feet of materials in these centers and hundreds of volumes chronically the Greek American experience.

Specific archival collections and their addresses may be obtained by contacting Ms. Mattheou at the above address.

HELLENIC COLLEGE AND HOLY CROSS ORTHODOX SCHOOL OF THEOLOGY 5C Goddard Avenue, Brookline, Massachusetts 02445. Founded in 1937 under the auspices of the Greek Orthodox Archdiocese in the Americas, it includes both college and seminary divisions for the training of priests for this church. The Cotsidas-Tonna Library on campus has 104,000 volumes including a collections on Byzantine history and hymnology and records of Greek families and parishes throughout the United States, Canada, and South America. It serves as the center of Greek cultural records and is open to researchers.

GREEK ORTHODOX ARCHDIOCESE OF AMERICA 8-10 East 79th Street, New York, New York 10021. This is the major religious body of Greek Americans representing more than two million members in some 600 parishes in nearly every state in the United States.

The Archdiocesan Chancery office holds many records of Greek church history in America. It is a valuable repository for those wishing to conduct research into Greek immigration patterns and settlement patterns in America.

Logo of the Greek Orthodox Archdiocese of America

THE ST. PHOTIOS NATIONAL SHRINE 41St. George Street, St. Augustine, Florida 32085-1960. This shrine is dedicated to the memory of the 1,403 Greek colonists from Smyrna in Asia Minor in 1768. The shrine consists of exhibits which depict the life of early Greek immigrants and the development of the Greek Orthodox Church in America as well as the beautiful St. Photios Chapel. A special A/V tape has been developed which creates a pictorial highway transporting the viewer from the shores of ancient Greece to America.

This is a good place for research into early family and parish histories, particularly of the Greek immigrants who came to the east coast of Florida.

Additional Greek Resources

American Hellenic Educational Progressive Assn (AHRPA),
1909 Q St. NW suite 500, Washington, DC 20009
Ph (202) 232-6300   www.ahepa.org

Boston Public Library, 666 Boylston, Boston, Mass 02117

Carnegie Public Library, 4400 Forbes, Pittsburgh, Pa 15217

Chian Federation of America, 4400 Broadway, Astoria, NY
11103
Ph. (718) 204-2550
www.chianfed.org

Cretans Association, 32 31st St., Astoria, NY 11106
Ph (718) 721-9172
www.nycretans.org

Cleveland Public Library, 325 Superior, Cleveland, Ohio
44103

Daughters of Penelope, 440 Whitehall Rd, Albany, NY
12208
Ph (510) 49-4442

Greek Archdiocese of N&S Amer., 8 E. 79th St., New York,
NY 10021

Greek Catholic Union, 5400 Tuscarawas Rd, Beaver, PA
15009
Ph (422) 495-3400
www.gccusa.com

Lowell Public Library, Marrimack Ave, Lowell, MA 01850

Manchester Public Library, 405 Pine St., Manchester, NH
03104

New Orleans Public Library, Loyola St., New Orleans, LA
70140

New York Public Library, 5th & 42nd, New York, NY 10018

Pan Arcadian Federation, 800 N. York Rd., Elmhurst, IL
 60126
Ph (630) 833-1900
www.panarcadian.org

Tarpon Springs Library, Orange Ave., Tarpon Springs, FL
 33501

United Hellenic American Congress, 980 N. Michigan
 Avenue, Chicago, Illinois 60611

Greek Bibliography

Burgess, Thomas Greeks in America, R&E Research 1970

Casavis, J. N. A Symposium on Dodecanese, Dodecaese
1938

Contopolous, Michael The Greek Community of New York,
Caratzas 1982

Cutsimbis, Michael A Bibliographical Guide, Migration Ctr.
1970

Georgakas, D. New Directions in Greek-Amer. Studies,
Pella 1991

Karas, Nicholas Greek Immigrants at Work, Metora 1987

Patterson, G. The Unassimilated Greeks of Denver, AMS
1989

Salcutos, Theodore Greeks in the U.S., Harvard UP 1964

Scurby, Alice The Greek Americans, Twayne Publ. 1984

Voultsos, Mary Greek Immigrant Passengers, H&E Books
1992

Zotos, Stephanos Hellenic Presence in America, Pilgrimage
1976

48

HUNGARIANS

Scattered records exist of the activities of Hungarian Americans throughout the colonial period and the first half of the 18th century. Hungary is a republic of central Europe with a population of 12 million who speak a Finno-Ugric language that is related to Finnish and Estonian.

While Hungarians served in both the Revolutionary and Civil Wars it wasn't until the 1880s that they began to arrive in large numbers in America. Some found employment in the coal mines of West Virginia and Pennsylvania as well as the grape orchards of Ohio and California. Others came to work in industrial centers such as Pittsburgh, Chicago, Detroit, Cleveland, and Youngstown, Ohio. A few also settled in small towns such as Beauty, Kentucky, a mining community and in Fairport Harbor, Ohio where Hungarians and Finns compose nearly the entire town.

While the majority of Hungarians are Roman Catholic and have ethnic parishes in many industrial cities, there are also significant numbers of Protestants, particularly in the Reformed, Presbyterian, and Lutheran denominations.

The Free Magyar Reformed Church in America was formed in 1922 and changed its name in 1958 to the Hungarian Reformed Church with a bishop headquartered near Detroit. It has 25 congregations which have a total of about 5,000 members. Within the Evangelical Lutheran Church in America there is a Hungarian Special Interest Conference with a President who is also a pastor of the denomination. Numerous Lutheran churches conduct services in the Hungarian language.

A small percentage of Hungarians are Jewish and there is a Hungarian Jewish Special Interest Group which has its Headquarters near Cleveland, Ohio.

There are about 700,000 Americans of Hungarian ancestry.

MAGYAR MARKETING

*Advertisement for a Hungarian interest
company in Youngstown, Ohio*

AMERICAN HUNGARIAN LIBRARY AND HISTORICAL SOCIEY 215 East 82nd Street New York, New York 10028. This library is open to the public for family and historical research every Thursday from 3 to 7 P.M . Under the direction of Dr. Otto Hamos, it contains volumes, documents, and tapes relating to Hungarian immigration and settlement in America, particularly in the eastern United States.

They welcome interested researchers in the field of Hungarian-American history. Ph. (212)249-9360 Website http://magyarhaz.org/index.php

Amerikai Magyar Könyvtár és Történelmi Társulat

215 EAST 82nd STREET, NEW YORK, N. Y. 10028

Letterhead American Hungarian
Library and Historical Society

Additional Hungarian Resources

American Hungarian Federation, 809 National Press Bldg., Washington, DC 20045
Ph. (202) 737-0127 Fax (202) 737-8 06
E-mail: info@americanhungarianfederation.org
Website www.americanhungarianfedcrntion.org

Hungarian American Friendship Society, 17327 W. Carmen Dr., Surprise, Arizona 85388
Ph. (916) 690-4293
Email: holmes@dholmes.com
Website www.dholmes.com.hafs.html

Hungarian Reformed Federation Of America, 2001 Mass Ave NW, Washington, DC 20036-1011
Ph. (202) 328-2630 Fax (202) 328-7984
E-mail: hrfa.org
Website www.hrfa.org

National Federation Of American Hungarians, 196 Hungaria Dr. Rockwood, PA 15557
Ph. (814) 352-7188 Fax (814)352-8002
E-mail: peter@harkay.com
Website www.hungarianfed-usa.org

Hungarian Special Interest Conference, Evangelical Lutheran Church (ELCA), 1467 Park Haven Row, Lakewood, Ohio 44107
Ph. (216) 221-3178 Fax (216) 227-9482
E-mail: amevko@sbcglobal.net

American Hungarian Folklore Centrum, 178 Oakdene Ave, Teaneck, NJ 07666
Ph. (201) 836-4869 Fax (201) 836-1590
E-mail: magyar@centrummanagment.org
Website http://magyar.org

Hungarian Bibliography

Bognar, Desi Hungarians in America, AFI Press 1972

Coke, W. F. The Magyars of Cleveland, Cofc 1919

Lengyel, Emil Americans From Hungary, Greenwood 1972

McGuire, Patrick Hungarian Texans, U of Texas Press 1993

Rezsue, G. Hungarians in America, Lerner 1969

Szesplaki, J. The Hungarians in America, Oceana 1974

Vardy, Steven The Hungarian American, Chelsea 1990

Wass, Albert Our Hungarian Heritage, Danubian 1975

LATVIANS

Latvia is the middle republic of the three Baltic nations bordered to the south by Lithuania and to the north by Estonia. All have recently become independent from the former Soviet Union. Latvian (or Lettish) is the language spoken. It is a very ancient language related to Sanskrit.

The first Latvians came to America with the Swedes in the 17th century when Livonia was a part of Sweden. Following the Russo-Japanese war of 1905, motivated by a desire to gain freedom from Russian demination, some Latvians came to American shores. However, it is difficult to determine their number since prior to World War I, Latvian immigrants were listed as Russians Germans, or Lithuanians.

Contrary to the usual tendency of other immigrant groups, the Latvians did not tend to form large settlements although they were concentrated in certain states and cities.

Nearly 50 percent of the total Latvian immigrants may be found in five cities: New York, Chicago, Boston, Philadelphia, and Baltimore. Some other areas also received small colonies including Senatobia, Mississippi and towns in Minnesota, New Jersey, and California.

In religion, the majority of Latvians are Lutheran, but there is also a sizeable number of Catholics, Baptists, Moravians and Eastern Orthodox. There are Latvian Lutheran parishes New York, Chicago, Seattle, Minneapolis, and Boston as well as Kalamazoo, Michigan which continue to offer services in the Latvian language. The Latvian Evangelical Lutheran Church in headquartered in Chicago and a paper is published in Brooklyn.

There are about 80,000 Americans of Latvian ancestry.

*Front cover of a Latvian- American
church periodical, published in the 1950s.*

LATVIAN EVANGELICAL LUTHERAN CHURCH IN AMERICA 2140 Orkla Drive, Golden Valley, Minnesota 55427-3432. The President of this organization is located in suburban Minneapolis and heads a church body of some 20,000 members in 72 congregations throughout both North and South America. Most members of this group are first and second generation Latvians who became refugees after the Second World War. Thus, the historical records of the Eastern European Baltic group do not go as far back as do many of the Slavic groups. However, it can still be a valuable resource for tracing both parish and family histories.

LATVIEŠU EVANGELISKI LUTERISKĀ BAZNĪCA AMERIKĀ
Prāvests/Dean Uldis Cepure, pārvaldes priekšnieks/President

Logo of the Latvian Evangelical Lutheran Church in America

LATVIAN STUDIES CENTER LIBRARY 1702. Fraternity Village Drive, Kalamazoo, Michigan 49006. Founded in 1983, the library has more than 25,000 volumes, 271 microfilms, 400 A-V tapes, 1,250 slides, and 115 maps relating to Latvia and the Latvian-American experience.

It serves as a valuable archival resource for those who are interested in doing research into the patterns of Latvian immigration and settlement in America.

Inventories to Personal Papers of Latvia
Americans: Raimunds Caks, Erik Dundurs, and
Leonids Slaucitajs
Comp. Astra Apsitis (first two, 1994) and Andris Straumanis
(third, 1980; reprinted); 1996.

Inventory to the Records of the Daugavas Vanagi-Minnesota and Daugavas Vanagi-ASV
Comp. Astra Apsitis in 1994; published 1996.
Records of the Minnesota branch and national Latvian Welfare Association (1956-1979).

Books on Latvian immigration to the U.S.

Additional Latvian Resources

Boston Public Library, 666 Boylston, Boston, MA 02117

Free Library of Philadelphia, Logan Square, Philadelphia, PA 19103

Kalamazoo Public Library. 315 S. Rose, Kalamazoo, MI 49007

Latvian Daugavas Vanagi, West Hood Ave., Chicago, IL 60660

Latvian Ev. Lutheran Church, 2140 Orkla Dr., Golden Valley, MN 55427

Latvian Society of Iowa, 2653 Grandview, Des Moines, IA 50317

Latvian Research, Rt 2 Box 1619A, McAllen, TX 78504-9802

Northwest Miss. Comm. College Library, Senatobia, Mississippi 38668

San Francisco Public Library, Civic Ctr, San Francisco, CA 94103

Seattle Genealogical Society, 8511 15th Ave NE, Seattle, WA 98111

American Latvian Association, 440 Hurley, Rockville, MD 20850

Latvian Bibliography

Bilmanis, Alfred History of Latvia, Greenwood 1969

Karklis, Maruta The J,atvians in America, Cceana 1974

Reed, Robert Finding Your Latvian-American Roots, R&E 1993

Roucek, Joseph Latvians in the U.S., Baltic 1936

Urck, R. Latvia, Country and People, Walter & Rapa 1949

LITHUANIANS

Lithuania is the southernmost republic of the three Baltic nations being bordered on the north by Latvia, on the south by Poland, and on the west by the Baltic Sea. Lithuania has about four million inhabitants who speak a language that is part of the Baltic-Slavic group of Indo-Germanic languages.

The first major Lithuanian immigration to the United States began about 1868. Some came to New England farms while many were lured by the agents of railway companies into Pennsylvania, particularly in the arthracite coal areas of Schuykill, Lucerne, and Lackawanna counties and in all the towns of the Wyoming valley of Pennsylvania.

Later waves of immigrants would settle in the major industrial centers, particularly Pittsburgh, Philadelphia, Detroit, Cleveland, and Chicago. There are also significant Lithuanian communities in smaller towns in Illinois, Wisconsin, and Michigan where residents are primarily engaged in farming.

The majority of Lithuanians are Roman Catholic in religion but there are also come Protestants among them, mainly Lutheran and Presbyterians.

Today there are about 100 Lithuanian Catholic parishes scattered throughout the nation which are composed of ethnic Lithuanians and use the Lithuanian language.

Among Protestant Lithuanians, the Lithuanian Evangelical Lutheran Church has a bishop and headquarters in Oak Park, Illinois.

The Marianapolis High School of Thompson, Connecticut is operated by the Lithuanian (Catholic) Marist Fathers.

There are about 300,000 American of Lithuanian ancestry.

LITHUANIAN RESEARCH & STUDIES CENTER 5620
South Claremont Avenue, Chicago, Illinois 60636. The
center was organized in 1982 with a goal of organizing and
sponsoring research on Lithanian and Lithuanian Americans
and to collect archival material and publish documents
relating to the people language, culture, and history of
Lithuania and Lithuanian Americans.

The archives contains more than 100,000 books, 1,600
periodicals titles, 300 video tapes, plus a large collection of
Lithuanian language newspapers, immigration, family, and
church records.

The education wing of the center trains teachers for
Lithuanian-background schools in the United States and the
Youth Center operates twenty-five separate programs. A
library staff is on duty to help those doing research.

BALZEKAS MUSEUM OF LITHUANIAN CULTURE 6500 S. Pulaski Road, Chicago, Illinois 60629-5136. For the past 33 years this museum has served as a repository for records of Lithuanian life, not only in the midwest, but throughout America. There are more than 40,000 volumes in its library including an outstanding genealogical collection.

In addition to cultural artifacts there is an art collection and a section of mediaeval suits of armor. The museum has 2,000 rare books, 1,000 audio tapes, 600 maps, 1,700 files of pamphlets and records, 12,000 files of manuscripts and more than 50,000 photographs which depict life in Lithuania as well as early immigrant life in America.

The museum and library rank among the finest resources of genealogical information of any ethnic group in America.

Additional Lithuanian Resources

Carnegie Library, 4400 Forbes, Pittsburgh, PA 15213

Chicago Public Library, 425 N. Michigan Ave, Chicago, IL
60606

Cleveland Public Library, 325 Superior, Cleveland, Ohio
44103

Detroit Public Library, 5201 Woodward, Detroit, MI 48202

Institute of Litguanian Studies, Woodside St., Arlington,
MA 02174

Lithuanian World Comm., Maplewood Ave, Chicago, IL
60629

Lithuanian Alliance, 307 W. 30th St., New York, NY 10001

Lithuanian Ev. Lutheran Church, 704 S. Claremont, Oak
Park, IL 60304

Lithuanian American Council, 6500 S. Pulaski, Chicago, IL
60629
Ph. (773) 735-6677
www.altcsnter.org

Lithuan Catholic Alliance, 71 S. Washington, Wilkes-Barre,
PA 18701
Ph (570) 823-3513
www.ipscu.org/lca

National Lithuanian Society of America, 9136 55th Street,
Oak Lawn, IL 60453
Ph. (708) 423-7871

Lithuanian Bibliography

Baskauskas, L. An Urban Enclave, AMS 1985

Bercovic, J. One New Shores, Appleton 1925

Budreckis, A. Lithuanians in America, Oceana 1976

Gedmintas, A. An Interesting Bit of Identity, AMS 1989

Greene, Victor For God and Country, Wisc. Hist. Soc 1973

King, J Lithuanian Families of Luzerne County, Pa K&K 1986

Reed, R. Finding Your Lithuanian-American Roots, R&E 1993

Roucek, Joseph American Lithuanians, Interpreter 1939

Vengris, V. Lithuanian Bookplates, Lithuanian Library 1980

Like most groups from Eastern Europe, the Poles are also more recent immigrants than those from northern Europe. Although Polish Americans were sprinkled throughout the thirteen colonies, migration on a large scale did not begin until the 1830s following a political uprising in their native land. Some colonies were founded in Texas, Wisconsin, and Michigan. Towns such as Polishville in Iowa, Pulaski in Missouri, Warsaw in North Dakota, Polonia in Texas and Krakow in Wisconsin all give testimony to the ethnic identity of their founders.

But the major cities received the bulk of Polish immigration with Chicago receiving more than one-half million. Detroit is close behind, followed by New York City. Other large cities which also have considerable Polish settlements include Milwaukee, Wisconsin; Jersey City and Newark, New Jersey; Cleveland, Ohio and Pittsburgh and Philadelphia. Many came to work in industries including textile mills in New England, the mines of Pennsylvania, the steel mills of Ohio and Indiana, the auto factories of Michigan, and the lumber camps of the Pacific.

The majority of Polish immigrants maintained membership in the Roman Catholic Church where they have established colleges and seminaries for the training of clergy including St. Mary's College and Theological Seminary in Orchard Lake, Michigan and St. Hyacinth College in Granby, Massachusetts. A few Poles have joined Protestant fellowships including those of the Baptist, Methodist, Episcopal, and Presbyterian Churches.

Some Poles belong to the Polish National Catholic Church which split from the Roman Catholic Church in 1904. They maintain the Savonarola Theological Seminary in Scranton, Pennsylvania.

There are an estimated 6,000,000 Americans of Polish descent.

Polish costumes display - Polish Museum in Chicago

MADONNA .UNIVERSITY LIBRARY 36600 Schoolcraft Road, Livonia, Michigan 48150-1173. Founded in 1947 by Polish Catholics, the library of the university has more than 126,000 volumes, 42 CD -ROM titles, and 13,000 AV: titles.

There are records of Polish immigration to the midwest including family histories and parish church archives. Maintained by a staff of professional librarians, the center offers opportunities for research.

Holy Mother of the Rosary Cathedral
BUFFALO, N.Y.

CENTER FOR POLISH STUDIES AND CULTURE St. Mary's College, 3535 Indian Trail, Orchard Lake, Michigan 48324-9908. St. Mary's College has roots dating back to 1879 when a Polish Catholic priest petitioned Pope Leo XIII for permission to establish a seminary for the training of priests. The Seminary of SS Cyril and Methodius started in Detroit in 1885. In 1909 it was moved to Orchard Lake and a college was established on the same campus in 1929.

In 1969 the Center for Polish Studies and Culture was founded and is .located in the Ark building on the campus. It has since accumulated a sizeable archive of American Polonia, plus Polish history.

It also houses a collection of rare books and manuscripts.

The Center staff is prepared to assist researchers. Those desiring special help are asked to call for an appointment.

Savonarola Theological Seminary

of the

Polish National Catholic Church

American Institute of Polish Culture
1440 79 St, Causeway - Suite 117, Miami, Florida 33141
Ph (305) 864-2349   www.ampolinstitute.org

Federation of Polish Americans
2000 L. St. NW - Suite 200, Washington, DC 20036
Fax (800) 486-4850   www.plishwashington.com/t:pa

Polish American Historical Society
1615 Stanley St., New Brittain, Connecticut 06050
Ph (800) 832-2808
www.polishamericanstudies.org

Polish Museum of America
984 N. Milwaukee Ave., Chicago, IL 60622-4101
Ph (773) 384-3352   www.pma.prcua.org

Polish Union of America
745 Center St., West Seneca, NY 14224
www.polishunion.com

Union of Poles in America
9999 Granger, Garfield Hts, Ohio 44125
Ph (216) 478-0120

Polish National Union of America
1002 Pittston Ave., Scranton, PA 18505
Ph (800) 724-6532   www.pna.org

Polish National Alliance
6100 N. Cicero Ave., Chicago, Illinois 60646
Ph (773) 26-0500   www.pnaznp.org

American Federation of Polish Jews
138 E 39th Street, New York, New York 10018
Ph (212) 689-4930

Alliance of Poles in America
6966 Broadway, Cleveland, OH 44105
Ph (216) 883-3131

KASUBIAN ASSOCIATION OF NORTH AMERICA P.O. Box 27732 Minneapolis, Minnesota 55427-0732. The Association exists to preserve Kashubian cultural heritage in North America and provide and encourage exchange with Kashubes in Poland. They desire to raise awareness of Kashubian ethnicity in North America and to stimulate an interest in Kashubian culture, in both Poland and America. Some genealogical records are maintained, research is encouraged, and a quarterly newsletter - Kashubian Association of North America Newsletter (KANA) is published on a quarterly basis.

Some professional genealogists who work with the Association will conduct research on family histories for a fee. This includes records that are both in Poland and in the United States.

Logo of the Kashubian Association

Additional Polish Resources

Carnegie Library, 4400 Forbes, Pittsburgh, PA15213

Chicago Public Library, 425 N. Michigan, Chicago, IL 60606

Cleveland Public Library, 325 Superior, Cleveland, OH 44103

Detroit Public Library, 5201 Woodward, Detroit, MI 48202

Jersey City Public Library, 72 Jersey Ave, Jersey City, NJ 07302

Manchester City Library, 405 Fine St., Manchester, NH 03104

Milwaukee Public Library, Wisconsin Ave, Milwaukee, WI 53233

New York Public Library, 5th & 42nd, New York, NY 10018

Polish Geneal. Society of Minnesota, 1650 Carroll, St. Paul, MN. 57104

Polish Geneal. Soc. of New York State, 299 Barnard, Buffalo, NY 14206

Polish Geneal. Soc of New England, 8 Lyle Rd., New Britain, CT 06053

Polish Geneal. Soc. of Wisconsin, Box 342341, Milwaukee, WI 53234

Polish Geneal. Soc. of Cleveland, 906 College, Cleveland, OH 44113

Polish Geneal. Soc. of Massachusetts, Box 381, Northampton, MA 01061

Polish Geneal. Soc of Detroit, 5201 Woodward, Detroit, MI 48202

Reuben McMillan Free Library, 350 Wick Ave, Youngstown, OH 44503

Scranton Public Library, Vine St., Scranton, PA 18503

Polish Bibliography

Baker, T. L. The Polish Texans, U of Texas Press, 1982

Borowec, Wlayer Ethnic Relations in Urban America, Polish-Amer 1938

Fox, Paul The Poles in America, Doubleday 1922

Gowaskio, J. The Polish Community in America, Franklin 1977

Kuniewski, Anthony Faith and Fatherland, Notre Dame 1980

Moscinski, Sharon Tracing Our Polish Roots, John Muir 1994

Obidinski, F. Polish Folkways in America, Polish American 1987

Paluszek, John Ari American Journey, American Ethnic 1981

Sanders, E. Polish-American Community Life, Polish Institute 1975

Toor, Richard The Polish Americans Chelsea 1988

Wytrwal, Joseph Behold the Polish American, Endurance 1977

ROMANIANS

The republic of Romania (also sometimes spelled Rumania) is situated on the Balkan Peninsula and has a population of about 20 million. Most of them speak Romanian which is a Romance language related to Italian and Spanish with both of whom it shares some ancient Latin roots. There are about 120,000 Romanian Americans.

Immigration from Romania began in the 1890s in significant numbers, although there had been a scattering of people prior to that time. The Romanians came primarily to large urban areas, particularly New York, Chicago, Cleveland, Pittsburgh, and Detroit. Smaller communities also came to Canton, Warren, and Youngstown, Ohio as well as to the Gary, Indiana area where they were drawn to job opportunities in the heavy industries of those cities.

Other Romanian immigrants went further west and established communities in Aurora, Illinois; Milwaukee, Wisconsin; Minneapolis, Minnesota; Portland, Oregon; as well as Los Angeles and San Francisco. There is also a large Romanian community in Miami, Florida.

About 70 percent of Romanians are Eastern Orthodox, with about 20 percent being Roman Catholic, and the remainder being Protestant or Jewish.

Eastern Orthodox Romanians are divided into the Romanian Orthodox Episcopate of America with a bishop and headquarters in Jackson, Michigan and the Romanian Orthodox Missionary Episcopate headquartered in Detroit. Together are about 100 parishes. Clergy are trained at the St. Vladimir's Orthodox Theological Seminary located in Yonkers, New York.

Among Roman Catholics there in a Byzantine-Romanian Eparchy whose bishop resides in Canton, Ohio. There are 11 such parishes, located mostly in northeastern Ohio.

ROMANIAN HERITAGE CENTER 2540 Grey Tower Road, Jackson, Michigan 49201-2208. The center was established in 1975 with support from the Romanian Orthodox Episcopate of America for the purpose of of providing a place where study and research could be conducted relating to Romanian immigration to America and Canada. It contains three major archival rooms with many church records, family correspondence, parish bulletins, and photographs. The library also contains Romanian newspapers of the United States and Canada, books about Romanian immigration, and numerous doctoral dissertations related to Romania and the Romanian-American experience.

ROMANIAN CULTURAL CENTER 200 East 38th Street, New York, New York 10016. The library of the Center contains about 23,000 books in both English and Romanian, plus many of the national and some of the local newspapers and magazines in Romanian.

There is a wide range of materials covering a large spectrum of Romanian and Romanian-American culture including literature, history, folklore, art music, theatre, cinema, science, etc.

The library is open to the public from 9 to 6 during; the week, but not on Saturdays or Sunday. The library holdings can be a valuable source of materials for those wishing to do research in Romanian-American immigration history. A librarian is on duty to assist.

ROMANIAN CULTURAL CENTER
NEW YORK
200 EAST 38TH STREET, NEW YORK, NY 10016

ROMANIAN ORTHODOX EPISCOPATE OF AMERICA 2522 Grey Tower Road, Jackson, Michigan 49201. The church was organized in 1929 and is now a diocese of the Orthodox Church of America (OJA). It serves as headquarters for Romanian Orthodox Christians throughout the United States and Canada with about 6,000 members in 34 parishes.

There is a close working relationship with the Romanian Heritage Center adjacent to church headquarters. There are parish and family records of Romanian communities nationwide.

A periodical, Solia, Romanian News is published.

**THE
ROMANIAN ETHNIC
ART MUSEUM**

Traditional pottery
Romanian Ethnic Art Museum, Cleveland, Ohio

THE ROMANIAN ETHNIC ART MUSEUM 3256 Warren Road, Cleveland, Ohio 44111. The museum is housed on the property of St. Mary's Romanian Orthodox .Church with whom it has maintained close ties since its inception in 1928.

In addition to many pieces of both secular and religious art, ranging from ceramic and metalwork to ecclesiastical vestments there is a large collection of Icons and paintings.

The museum maintains a library of about 6,000 books relating to life in Romania as well as family and parish histories of Romanian immigrants to the Cleveland area and its vicinities.

ROMANIAN ORTHODOX CHURCH IN AMERICA 19959 Riopelle, Detroit, Michigan 48203. This church was organized as a diocese in 1929 with headquarters and cathedral in Detroit and includes parishes in both the United States and Canada. Until 1950 it was known as the Romanian Orthodox Missionary Episcopate. It has 30 parishes, over half of which are located in Canada, but some also in the United States in New York, Pennsylvania, Ohio, and Michigan.

The headquarters has records of Romanian-American families and parishes and can serve as a resource for those researching Romanian-American immigration history.

ST. MARY'S ROMANIAN ORTHODOX CHURCH 3256 Warren Road, Cleveland, Ohio 44111. This in the oldest Romanian Orthodox church in the United States. The parish library has about 2,000 volumes with parish and family archives going back: as far as 1904.

The archives serves as an excellent source for genealogical materials relating to Romanian immigration to the Cleveland and northeastern Ohio area.

There is also a Romanian Ethnic Arts Museum adjacent to the church and parish hall which is open to the public.

St. Mary's Romanian Orthodox Church Cleveland

Romanian Studies Institute of America
6937 Bay Drive - Suite 210
Miami, Florida 33141
Ph (305) 994-1419
www.umo.ca/modiang/rsaa

Society for Romanian Studies
Huntington College
Department of History
Huntington, Indiana 46750
Ph (260) 359-4242
Fax (260) 356-4086
www.huntington.edu/srs

Union and League or Romanian Societies
7805 Brookpark Rd.
Parma, Ohio 44129-1111
Ph (216) 351-2094
Fax (216) 351-2094

American Friends of Romania
P. O. Box 5884
Bethesda, Maryland 20824
Ph (202) 966-1922
www.afromoc@yahoo.com

Additional Romanian Resources

Carnegie Library, 4400 Forbes, Pittsburgh, PA 15213

Chicago Public Library, 425 N. Michigan, Chicago, IL 60606

Cleveland Public Library, 325 Superior, Cleveland, OH 44103

Detroit Public Library, 5201 Woodward, Detroit, MI 48202

New York Public Library, 5th & 42nd, New York, NY 10018

Stark County District Library, 715 Market Ave, Canton, Ohio 44702

Youngstown Public Library, 350 Wick, Youngstown, OH 44503

Warren Trumbull County Library, 444 Mahoning, Warren, OH 44483

Romanian Bibliography

Andronescu, S. Who's Who in Romanian America, Amer. Instit 1979

Condrescu , Andrei Disappearance of the Outside. Addison-Wesley 1990

Diamond, Arthur The Romanian American, Chelsea 1988

Galitzi, Christine A Study of Assimilation, AMS 1980

Manuila, V. Social Background of the Romanian Immigrant, Family 1975

Wersmann, Valdimir Romanians in America, Oceana 1980

Russians arrived in America from both east and west. In the late 1700s numerous Russian colonies were established in Alaska, from which they spread south to California. Migration into the United States from Alaskan territory was constant, although for a while it was only in small numbers. Gradually San Francisco and Los Angeles became centers for them.

Easterm immigration came later, beginning slowly in the 1820s and increasing; gradually into the 1870s. Many more came in the 1920s as a result of the Russian revolution and by the 1940s there were nearly 600,000 Americans of Russian ancestry.

The largest number of Russian immigrants were members of the Russian Orthodox Church which was divided into three jurisdictions namely the Russian Orthodox Greek Catholic Church, the Russian Orthodox Church in the USA & Canada, and the Russian Orthodox Church Outside Russia. There was also the Byelorusaian Autocephalic Orthodox Church. Concentrations of Russians were mainly in large cities as New York, Pittsburgh, Boston, Chicago, and Minneapolis.

There are also a few Russian Catholic parishes in the eastern United States plus some affiliated with Protestant groups including the Molokans who settled in California, the Doukhobors who migrated from Canada to Los Angeles and San Diego, and the Old Believers who came to the town of Essen near Pittsburgh.

The largest number of Russian Americans reside in Pennsylvania while Connecticut, New Jersey, New York, and Ohio also have many. Many work in the industrial settings of major cities, but some are also employed in the coal mines of Pennsylvania, Ohio, and West Virginia.

Russians maintain three theological seminaries for the training of priests for the Russian Orthodox Church. These are St. Tikhon's Seminary at South Canaan, Pennsylvania, Holy Trinity Orthodox Seminary at Jordanville, New York, and St. Vladimir's Orthodox Theological Seminary at Yonkers, New York.

St. Michael's Russian Orthodox Greek Catholic Church

512 Summer Street   Tel. (717) 457-3703

OLD FORGE, PA. 18518

MUSEUM OF RUSSIAN CULTURE 2450 Sutter Street, San Francisco, California·94115. The earliest Russian migration to North America came by way of Alaska where Russian colonies were established in the 1790s. A half century later there would be southward movement, particularly to California where the city of San Francisco became a center of Russian colonization. The museum, under the direction of Dimitri Brown, contains more than 17,000 volumes which chronicle early Russian history on the west coast, including information on the first Russian Orthodox Chapel built at Fort Ross in 1812. This is an excellent library and museum for resources materials on that early period.

ST. VLADIMIR'S ORTHODOOX THEOLOGICAL SEMINARY 575 Scarsdale Road, Yonkers, New York 10707. This seminary was established in 1938 to train priests for service in the Russian Orthodox Church. The Father Georges Florovsky Library is part of the seminary complex and contains 94,000 volumes including special collections of Byzantine history and art as well as Russian theology and history.

As an academic library, its primary focus is not genealogical, but it does have significant holdings on the history and culture of Russian Orthodox parishes and families in the United States including 1350 microfiche and 600 films in its collection.

ST. VLADIMIR'S ORTHODOX THEOLOGICAL SEMINARY

HOLY TRINITY ORTHODOX SEMINARY P.O. Box 36, Jordanville, New York 13361-0036. This seminary was founded in 1948 by the Most Rev, Archbishop Vitaly for the purpose of training priests for the Russian Orthodox Church.

The seminary library contains more than 36,000 volumes focusing on Eastern Orthodox theology and Russian studies.

While not intended to be a prime source of genealogical information it, nevertheless has numerous documents relating to early Russian Orthodox families and parish particularly those located in the North eastern United States and may, therefore be of some assistance to the researcher of Russian-American history.

Holy Trinity
Orthodox Seminary

ST. TIKRON'S ORTHODOX THEOLOGICAL SEMINARY Post Office Box 130, South Canaan, Pennsylvania 18459. This school has been a training institution for priests of the Russian Orthodox Church for more than 60 years.

The library has 24,000 volumes relating to Orthodox theology, spirituality, and liturgics with a special collection of Russian and Old Slavonic theological and literary materials.

While not primarily a genealogical repository, the library does have material on early parish and family records and should not be overlooked in any study of Russian immigrant history.

ST. HERMAN'S ORTHODOX THEOLOGICAL SEMINARY 414 Mission Road, Kodiak, Alaska 99615. The seminary library and archives house a priceless record of Russian activity in Alaska dating back to the mid-eighteenth century. Nearby Holy Resurrection Cathedral was established in 1795.

The library also contains 5,500 volumes including many works in the Russian language. This is a great source of historical information on Russian history in Alaska.

Logo of St. Herman's

Belarusian Institute of Arts and Science
166-34 Gothic Drive
Jamaica, New York 11432
Ph (201) 244-0776 Fax (732) 557-0095

North American Assn for Belarisian Studies Harvard Univ.
12 Quincy St.
Cambridge, Massachusetts 92138-3804
www.belarusianstudies.org

Congress of Russian Americans
2160 Sutter St.
San Francisco, California 94115
Ph (415) 928-5841
www.russian-americans.org

Orthodox Society of America
29510 Lorain Road
North Olmsted, Ohio 44070-3909
Ph (440) 716-2360
www.lcba.com/about/aboutosa.htm

Russian Brotherhood Organization
1733 Spring Garden St.
Philadelphia, Penna 19130
Ph (215) 563-2537
www.rbo.org

Russian Orthodox Catholic Mutual Aid Society
10 Down Street
Wilkes-Barre, Penna 18705-3802
Ph (570) 882-8591
www.rocmas.org

Tolstoy Foundation
P. O. Box 578
Valley Cottage, New York 10989
Ph (845) 2686722 www.tolstoyfoundation.org

Additional Russian Resources

Alaska Historical Society Library, State Office Building, Juneau, Alaska 99811

Allentown Public Library, Hamilton Hall, Allentown, PA 18102

Boston Public Library, 666 Boylton. Boston, MA 02117

Carnegie Library, 4400 Forbes, Pittsburgh, PA 15213

Chicago Public Library, 425 N. Michigan, Chicago, IL 60606

Cleveland Public Library, 325 Superior, Cleveland,OH 44103

New York Public Library, 5th & 42nd, New York, NY 10018

Youngstown Public Library, 350 Wick, Youngstown, OH 44503

Russian Orthodox Church Outside Russia, 75 E. 93rd, New York, NY 10028

Russian Orthodox Church in the USA, 15 E. 97th, New York, NY 10029

San Francisco Public Library, Civic Ctr., San Francisco, CA 94115

St. Hermans Theological Seminary Library, Kodiak, AK 99615

Scranton Public Library, Vine Street, Scranton, PA 18503

University of Pittsburgh Library, 5th & Forbes, Pittsburgh, PA.15260

Russian Bibliography

Davis, Jerome The Russian Immigrant, Macmillan 1922

Eubank, Nancy Russians in America, Lerner 1972

Federova, S. Russian Population in Alaska, Cal. Limestone 1973

Johnston, Barry Russian-American Social Mobility, Cent 21 1981

Magosci, Paul The Russian Americans, Chelsea 1989

Pierce, Richard Russian American, Limestone 1990

Reed, R. Finding Your Russian-American Roots, R&E 1993

Saroyan, W. Hilltop Russians in San Francisco, Stanford 1941

Wertsmann, Valdimir The Russians in America, Oceana 1977

SERBIANS

Serbia is one of the republics of the former Yugoslavia with a population of about nine million. Unlike neighboring Slovenia and Croatia, which are largely Roman Catholic the Serbs arc primarily Eastern Orthodox. The principle language is Serbo-Croatian, but Serbs use the Cyrillic alphabet related to Russian while the Croatians use the Roman alphabet.

Serbs began coming to America through the port of New Orleans in the 18th century and later left for the California gold rush. On the Pacific coast they became involved in the apple, grape, and fishing industries.

The bulk of Serbian immigration to America did not come until the late 19th century and continued well into the 20th. These groups tended to cluster in the major industrial areas where they worked in factories and mills. The cities of Pittsburgh, Detroit, Chicago, Cleveland, and Youngstown, Ohio received large numbers of Serbian immigrants.

The majority of Serbs remained in the Eastern Orthodox Church and established the Serbian Orthodox Church in the United States of America and Canada which is divided into three major dioceses - the Eastern American and Canadian, headquartered in Cleveland, Ohio; the Mid-West Diocese headquartered in Chicago; and the Western Diocese headquartered in Alhambra, California all together having a total of about 90 parishes. This church also maintains the St. Sava's Monastery in Libertyville, Illinois. Many of its priests are trained at the St. Vladimir's Orthodox Theological Seminary in Yonkers, New York.

In addition to the concentrations in the industrial and metropolitan areas mentioned, there are also scattered communities in Minnesota, Montana, Missouri, Nebraska, Kansas, and Texas with cathedrals in New York City and Milwaukee.

There are about 250,000 Americans of Serbian ancestry.

THE IMMIGRATION HISTORY RESEARCH CENTER University of Minnesota, 826 Berry Street, St. Paul, Minnesota 55114. This is one of the nation's leading archival/library repositories of source material on immigration and ethnicity. The IHRC locates, collects, preserves, and makes available for research the records of Serbian immigration as well as twenty-three other eastern European ethnic groups.

The print collection consists of 25,000 books and pamphlets, more than 3,000 serial titles, and over 900 newspaper titles. Most of these are the products of the ethnic presses in the United States and Canada from the late 19th century to the present.

There are also personal papers of community leaders, clergy, journalists, and educators. Additional materials consist of many photographs, videotape recordings and oral history audiotape recordings.

THE IMMIGRATION HISTORY
RESEARCH CENTER A BRIEF PROFILE

The Logo of the IHRC

Serbian National Defense Council of America
5782 N. Elston Street
Chicago, Illinois 60646-5546
Ph (773) 775-7772
Fax (77)775-7779
www.snd-us.com

Serb National Federation
One Fifth Ave - 7th Floor
Pittsburgh, Penna. 15222
Ph (412) 642-7372
Fax (412) 642-1372
www.serbnatlfco.org

Macedonian-American Friendship Association
57 Jefferson Ave
Columbus, Ohio 43215
Ph (614) 668-9656
Fax (614) 457-5926
www.macedonianamerican.org

Macedonian Patriotic Organization
124 W. Wayne St.
Ft. Wayne, Indiana 46802
Ph (260) 422-5900
Fax (260) 422-1348
www.macedonian.org

Additional Serbian Resources

Alhambra Public Library, 401 W. Main, Alhambra, CA
   91801

Carnegie Library, 4400 Forbes, Pittsburgh, PA 15213

Chicago Public Library, 425 N. Michigan, Chicago, IL
   60606

Cleveland Public Library, 325 Superior, Cleveland, OH
   44103

Detroit Public Library, 5201 Woodward, Detroit, MI 48202

Youngstown Public Library, 350 Wick Ave. Youngstown,
   OH 44503

St. Sava' s Monastery, Libertyville, IL 60505

Serbian Orthodox Church, 5701 Redwood, Chicago, IL
   60656

Serbian National Committee, West North Ave., Chicago, IL
   60647

Serbian National Fed., 3414 5th Ave., Pittsburgh, PA 15213

Serbian Bibliography

Colacovic, B. Yugoslav Migration to America, Ragusan 1973

Goverchin, Gerald Americans From Yugoslavia, Ragusan 1961

Ifkevic, Edward The Yugoslavian American, Lerner 1971

Kisslinger, Jerome The Serbian Americans, Chelsea 1990

Padgett, Deborah Settlers and Sojourners, AMS 1969

SLOVAKS

The Slovak Republic or Slovakia, constitutes the eastern third of the former Czechoslovakia and has about five million people. There are also Carpatho-Rusyns, Hungarian, and Ukrainian minorities.

The majority of Slovak immigration to American shores occurred in the 19th century. They were drawn to job opportunities in Pittsburgh, Chicago, and Cleveland, but they also developed scattered communities in Illinois, Wisconsin, Arkansas, Florida, and Texas. Their ethnic identity remains on such towns as Slovaktown, Arkansas and Slavia and Masaryktown, both in Florida.

About one-half of the Slovaks who came to the United States remained in the Roman Catholic Church, but significant numbers were also Eastern Orthodox (Carratho-Rusyn) and various Protestant groups, primarily Lutheran and Presbyterian. The sisters of the Order of Cyrillius and Methodius of Danville, Pennsylvania has been instrumental in providing elementary and secondary school teachers and the Slovak Roman Catholic Union with more than 100,000 members, has given birth to numerous religious schools among the Slovak population in the United States.

Among Protestant Slovaks there was, until the 1950s, a Slovak Calvinistic Presbyterian Union in Pennsylvania which has now been integrated into general Presbyterian work. A self-governing Slovak Synod of the Lutheran Church with 20,000 members, recently united with the larger Lutheran Church-Missouri Synod. Also the Evangelical Lutheran Church in America continues to maintain a Slovak Zion Synod with a bishop who is headquartered in Chicago.

Immigration from the Carpatho-Rusyn area of Slovakia brought many of the Eastern Orthodox faith to this nation and helped to establish the American Carpatho-Russian Orthodox Greek Catholic Church. It maintains a diocesan headquarters in Johnstown, Pennsylvania which is also the home of its Christ the Saviour Seminary.

THE NATIONAL CZECH AND SLOVAK MUSEUM AND LIBRARY 30 16th Avenue SW, Cedar Rapids, Iowa 52404. The museum and library was established in 1973 for the purpose of preserving Czech and Slovak heritage. It is a rich treasury of historical records dating back to early immigration in eastern Iowa (the 1850s) when the first parish churches were established. In addition to parish and family records there is a sizeable collection of arts works, printing presses, musical instruments and numerous other objects of historical interest.

SLOVAK MUSEUM AND ARCHIVES 1011 Rosedale Avenue, Middletown, Pennsylvania 17057. This museum and archives is maintained by the First Catholic Slovak Union (Jednota) of America which was founded by Father Stephen Furdek in Cleveland, Ohio in 1890. The archives constitute a rich resource for family and parish histories of Slovak immigrants. There is a collection of rare books plus almanacs, newspapers, periodicals, commemorative pamphlets, documents and photographs relating to early Slovak history in America. There are also papers and letters of men and women who wore prominent in Slovak religion and fraternal life.

There are more than 3,000 books in Slovak, English, and otter languages on history, art, music, literature, science, and religion.

The staff of the archives invites scholars in Sloval family history to make use of their research files.

CHRIST THE SAVIOUR SEMINARY 225 Chandler Street Johnstown, Pennsylvania 15906. The seminary was founded in 1940 by Bishop Orestes P. Chornock of the American Carpatho-Russian Greek Orthodox Church for the purpose of training priests to serve in that church. Its ministry is primarily who came to the United States from the Carpathian Mountain area of eastern Slovak and speak a language related to both Sloval and Russian. The library has more than 5,000 volumes including historical documents related to parish and family records of the Carpatho-Russian peoples in America, particularly in the Pennsylvania, Ohio, and New York regions.

First Catholic Slovak Union
6611 Rockdale Road
Independence, Ohio 44131
Ph (216) 642-9406
www.fcsu.cmo

National Slovak Society
351 Valley Brook Rd.
McMurray, Penna 15317-3337
Ph (721) 731-0094 Fax (724)731-0145
www.nssslife.org

Slovak Catholic Federation
408 N. Main St.
Taylor, Penna 18517-1108
Ph (570) 698-5584 www.slovakcatholicfederation.org

Slovak Catholic Sokol
205 Madison Street
Passaic, New Jersey 07055
Ph (800) 886-7656 www.slovakcatholicsokol.org

Slovak American Cultural Center
P.O. Box 5395
New York, New York 10185
E-Mail: info@slovakamericancc.org

Slovak Studies Association University of Illinois
361 Lincoln Hall, 702 S. Wright St.
Urbana, Illinois 61801
Ph (217) 244-7270
www.asuky.edu.ssa

First Catholic Slovak Ladies Association
24950 Chagrin Bld.
Brentwood, Ohio 44122-5634
Ph (216) 464-8015 Fax (216) 464-9260
www.fcsla.com

Additional Slovak Resources

Carnegie Library, 44400 Forbes, Pittsburgh, PA 15213

Chicago Public Library, 425 N. Michigan, Chicago, IL 60606

Cleveland Public Library, 325 Superior, Cleveland, OH 44103

Milwaukee Public Library, 814 W. Wisconsin, Milwaukee, WI 53233

Youngstown Public Library, 350 Wick, Youngstown, OH 44503

Scranton Public Library, Vine St., Scranton, PA 18503

Slovak Zion Synod - Lutheran Church, 8340 N. Oleander, Niles, IL 60714-2552

Slovak Catholic Sokol, Madison St., Passaic, NJ 07055

The Carpatho-Rusyn Knowledge Base, P. O. Box 3339, Davisburg, MI 48350-0339

The Carpatho-Rusyn Research Center, Box 1313, Orwell, VT 05760

The Rusin Instit. Of Minnesota, 1115 Pineview, Plymouth, MN 55441

The Carpatho-Rusyn Society, 125 Westland Dr., Pittsburgh, PA 15217

Slovak and Rusyn Roots, 123 Baywood, Boulder Creek, CO 95006

Slovak Bibliography

Magosci, Paul Carpatho-Rusyn America, Chelsea 1993

Stan, H. An Ethno-Historical Study of Slovak Amer, Ayer 1981

Stein, H. Ethno-Historic Study of Slovak Amer., Amer 8th Gr. 1981

Stolarik, Mark The Slovak American, Chelsea House 1988

Stolarik, Mark Growing Up On The South Side, Bucknell UP 1985

Roucek, Joseph Czechs and Slovaks in America, Lerner 1967

SLOVENIANS

Slovenia is the northernmost republic of the former Yugo-slavin nation. There are about two million Slovenians who speak the Slovenian language which is a Slavic tongue. Many Slovenians also speak Serbo-Croatian.

Slovenians began migrating to America in the middle of the 19th century settling originally in such northern industrial cities as Pittsburgh, Detroit, Chicago, Cleveland and Youngstown, Ohio being: drawn to many job opportunities that existed in heavy industries such as iron and steel and large machinery. This represented a somewhat radical change in type of employment for most of them since many had been employed in the agricultural trades back in their native land.

In addition to these industries, Slovenian immigrants also found employment as masons, longshoreman, and lumberman. Only a few actually found employment in agricultural works and those were chiefly the ones who migrated to the Pacific Northwest and chose farming as their occupation. Others who made the trip across America found work in the great fishing industries that dotted the Pacific coast.

Slovenian-Americans are mainly Roman Catholic by religion.

The First Slovenian church was established in 1871 in Brockway, Minnesota. They continue to maintain Roman Catholic congregations which minister in the Sloveian language and are under the jurisdiction of the bishops of the various dioceses in the United States. There are about 70 such parishes in America.

There are about 300,000 Americans of Slovenian ancestry.

Historic St. Josephs Slovenian Church

THE SLOVENIAN HERITAGE MUSEUM 431 North Chicago Street, Joliet, Illinois 60432. The Union was founded in 1926 by Marie Prisland to foster cooperation among Slovenian immigrants in the new world, particularly women, who help found the museum in 1983.

The Museum contains valuable collections of Slovenian history and culture in America including Slovenian churches and parish families. As such the Museum has become a resource center for students of Slovenian immigration to the United States.

There is a sizeable photographic collection and many artifacts including household items, prayer books, wedding gowns, and clotting worn by early settlers.

There are also videos which trace the history of Slovenian migration and its pioneer leaders as well as the leaders of the Slovenian-Women's-Union and a collection of early newspapers in the Slovenian language.

SLOVENIAN GENEALOGICAL SOCIETY INTERNATIONAL HEADQUARTERS 52 Old Farm Road, Camp Hill, Pennsylvania 17011-2604. The Society was established to coordinate research efforts into Slovenian genealogical research. It has chapters in California, Colorado, Florida, Kansas, Missouri, Maryland, Ohio, Oklahoma, Oregon, Texas, and Wisconsin, in addition to ones in Canada and Australia.

This is an excellent repository for those wishing to trace immigration patterns, the development of parishes and communities, as well as family histories.

The Society also publishes a quarterly Newsletter.

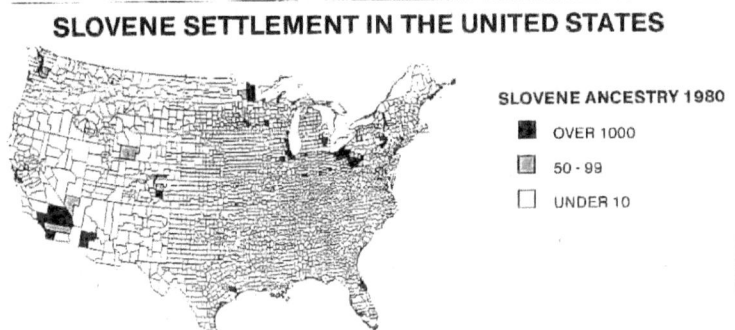

SLOVENE SETTLEMENT IN THE UNITED STATES

SLOVENE ANCESTRY 1980

■ OVER 1000

▨ 50 - 99

☐ UNDER 10

Map of Slovenian settlements in America
Courtesy of the Slovenian Women s Union

AMERICAN SLOVENIAN CATHOLIC UNION 2439 Glenwood Avenue, Joliet, Illinois 60435. The Union was founded by Slovenian immigrants as a nonprofit fraternal organization to provide financial security and family benefits to members nationwide. There are also valuable historical records relating to both families and parishes.

The Union is divided into 5 federations: the Illinois Federation with chapters in Chicago, Joliet, and Waukegan; the Minnesota Federation with chapters in Duluth, Hibbing, Ely, and Tower; the Ohio, including Cleveland, Girard, Lorain, and Barberton; Western Pennsylvania including Pittsburgh and Aliquippa; and the Wisconsin Federation including Milwaukee and Sheboygan.

In addition there are lodges with historical records in Pueblo, Colorado; Indianapolis, Indiana; Anaconda, Montana; St. Louis, Missouri; Bridgeport, Connecticut; Kansas City, Kansas; and San Francisco, California.

JOHN GORNICK SLOVENIAN LIBRARY AND ST. MARY'S MUSEUM OF RELIGIOUS HISTORY 211 East Nesa Ave, Pueblo, Colorado 84007. This institution was founded in 1969 and contains sizeable holdings of genealogy of Slovenian families who came to America as well as histories of Slovenian Catholic parishes in the United States.

A library of some 800 books is maintained, many of which are written in the Slovenian language as well as other languages of the former Yugoslavia.

The Museum also contains some very old tools which were made in Slovenia plus some church artifacts and Slovenian magazines which date back more than a century.

JOHN GORNICK
SLOVENIAN
HERITAGE
LIBRARY

JOHN GORNICK SLOVENIAN LIBRARY
and
ST. MARY'S MUSEUM
OF
RELIGIOUS HISTORY

LOCATED AT
211 EAST MESA AVE
PUEBLO, COLORADO

Logo of the Library & Museum

Additional Slovenian Resources

Carnegie Library, 4400 Forbes, Pittsburgh, PA 15223

Chicago Public Library, 425 N. Michigan, Chicago, IL 60606

Cleveland Public Library, 325 Superior, Cleveland, OH 44103

Detroit Public Library, 5201 Woodward, Detroit, MI 48202

Youngstown Public Library, 350 Wick Ave., Youngstown, OH 44503

Scranton Public Library, Vone Street, Scranton, PA 18503

Slovenian Women's Union, 1131 Chicago St., Joliet, IL 60432

Slovenian Bibliography

Arnel, J. A Slovenian Community in Bridgeport, Ct, Slovenica 1971

Bennett, L Croats and Slovens in Wash. D. C. Ragusan 1978

Colacovic, B. Yuoslav Migration to America, Ragusan 1973

Dwyer, Joseph Slovenes in the U. S. and Canada, Immigr. Hist. 1981

Govorchin, Gerald Americans From Yugoslavia, Ragusan 1961

Ifkovic, Edward The Yugoslavian Americans, Lerner 1971

UKRAINIANS

The term, Ukrainian, also includes Ruthenians and sometimes Carpatho-Rusyns dependiug on the area from which they migrated. Regardless they are tied together by a common language and by a common religious experience, while early records indicate the presence of Ukrainians in colonial times, the actual history of Ukrainian immigration began in the 1870s when large numbers migrated to the great industrial centers of Pittsburgh, Detroit, Chicago, Cleveland and Youngstown, Ohio.

Pittsburgh and southwestern Pennsylvania has the largest con of Ukrainian settlers in America where they came to work in the steel industry and Scranton-Wilkes Barre area in northeastern Pennsylvania where they came to work in the coal mines. In addition, there are significant numbers in Philadelphia, in Stamford, Connecticut, and in the New Jersey cities of Patterson, Passaic, Elizabeth, and New Brunswick. Some Ukrainian American also work in farming communities in such places as Kiev and Russo in North Dakota; Scobey, Montana; and Chisholm, Minnesota.

Many Ukrainians are members of Eastern Orthodox Churches, particularly the Ukrainian Orthodox Church of America, the Ukrainian Orthodox Church of the USA, and the Holy Ukrainian Autocephalic Orthodox Church in Exile, all of which comprise more than 125 congregations.

Other Ukrainians affiliated with various Roman Catholic jurisdictions including the Parma Ohio Byzantine, the Passaic New Jersey Eparchy, the Philadelphia Archeparchy, the Pittsburgh Byzantine, the St. Nicholas of Chicago, the Van Nuys Byzantine, and the Christ the Redeemer Byelorussian parish in Chicago.

Clergy for Byzantine Catholic parishes are trained at the Ukrainian Seminary of St. Basil's College in Stamford, Connecticut, at Josaphat' s Seminary in Washington, DC, and at the Saints Cyril and Methodius Seminary near Pittsburgh.

There are an estimated 850,000 persons of Ukranian ancestry in America.

UKPAINIAN NATIONAL, ASSOCATITON 2200 Route 10, P. O. Box 280, Parsippany, New Jersey 07051. The Association was founded in 1894 in Shamokin, Pennsylvania and is primarily a fraternal benefit organization which attempts to meet the insurance and educational needs of thousands of Ukrainian-Americans.

Since its beginnings in 1894 the Association has published Svoboda, a Ukrainian-language newspaper, as well as a paper called the Ukrainian Weekly in English.

An extensive library and archives are maintained and all back issues of these periodicals are on microfiche, thus making them a valuable resource for the researcher of historical information regarding families, parish churches and communities of Ukrainian settlement in America.

UKRAINIAN NATIONAL ASSOCIATION, Inc.
УКРАЇНСЬКИЙ НАРОДНИЙ СОЮЗ, Інк.

2200 Route 10, P.O.Box 280, Parsippany, NJ 07054
Tel: (973) 292-9800, Ext. 3071 (800) 253-9862, Fax: (973) 292-0900

Since 1894

OKSANA TRYTJAK
UNA
Special Projects Coordinator

Logo of the Ukrainian National Association

IMMIGRATION HISTORY RESEARCH CENTER University of Minnesota, 826 Berry Street, St. Paul, Minnesota 55114-1076. The IHRC, founded in 1965, is an international resource on American immigration and ethnic history. The Center promotes the study and appreciation of ethnic pluralism through an active program of archival collection development, publications, conferences, lectures, and exhibits.

In addition to extensive Ukrainian Resources there are also materials relating to many other Eastern European groups, particular Slovenian, Polish, Greek, and Serbian.

A staff of trained professionals is maintained to assist the family history researcher.

Ukrainians in North America,
A Select Bibliography
Comp. Halyna Myroniuk and Christine Worobec; with the Multicultural History Society of Ontario, 1981.

A Guide to Ukrainian American Newspapers
in Microform
Comp. Halyna Myroniuk and Alexander Lushnycky; 1998.

Provides places, years, and other details of publication of early Ukrainian American newspapers available on microfilm at the IHRC and the Schevchenko Scientific Society (co-publishers).

Two Ukrainian-American historical publications provided by the press of the IHRC

BYZANTINE CATHOLIC SEMINARY OF SAINTS CYRIL AND METHODIUS 3605 Perrysville Avenue, Pittsburgh, Pennsylvania 15214. This school was established in 1950 to train priests of the Byzantine Rite and is maintained by the Byzantine Rite dioceses of Passaic and Parma and the archdiocese of Munhall, with ethnic backgrounds of Hungarian, Ruthenian, and Ukrainian.

While not primarily a genealogical repository, the library of more than 28,000 volumes has family and parish history records relating to the early days of these three immigrant groups.

The Dome of SS Cyril and Methodius Seminary Church

UKRAINIAN MUSEUM ARCHIVES LIBRARY 1202 Kenilworth, Cleveland, Ohio 44113. The museum library houses more than 17,000 volumes relating both to the history of the Ukraine and to Ukrainian-American history and culture.

It is an excellent resource institution for those wishing to study the historical background of Ukrainian immigration to the new world.

There are also special collections such as the Taras Shevchenko Ukrainian Revolution Collection and the large Ukrainian Religion Periodical Collection outside of the Ukraine with holdings dating back to 1900 and continuing to the present day.

Additional Ukrainian Resources

Allentown Public Library, Hamilton Mall, Allentown, PA 18102

Carnegie Library, 4400 Forbes, Pittsburgh, PA 15213

Chicago Public Library, 425 N. Michigan, Chicago, IL 60606

Cleveland Public Library, 325 Superior, Cleveland, OH 44503

Detroit Public Library, 5201 Woodward, Detroit, MI 48202

Fox Chase Manor, 701 Fox Chase Rd, Jenkintown, PA 19111

Free Library of Philadelphia, 1901 Vine, Philadelphia, PA 19107

Judas Magnes Library, 291 Russell St., Berkeley, CA 94701

New York Public Library, 5th & 42nd, New York, NY 10018

Youngstown Public Library, 350 Wick Ave, Youngstown, OH 44503

Scranton Public Library, Vine St., Scranton, PA 18503

Ukrainian Fraternal Assn, 440 Wyoming Ave., Scranton, PA 18503

Ukrainian Orthodox Church, P. O. Box 495, S. Bound Brook, NJ 08880

Ukrainian Bibliography

Duhovy, Andrew Pilgrims of the Prairie, Ukr. Cult. Instit. 1994

Gambal, M. Our Ukrainian Background, Workingmans Assn 1936

Halich, Wasyl Ukrainians in the United States, Arno 1970

Kuropas, Myron Ukrainians in America, Lerner 1972

Kuropas, Myron Ukrainian America, U. of Toronto 1991

Magessi, P. The Ukrainian Experience in the US, Harvard UP 1979

Osborn, Kevin The Ukrainian Americans, Chelsea 1989

Renoff, R. Carpatho-Russian Immigration, Harvard UP 1975

Subtelny, O. Ukrainians in North America, U. of Toronto 1991

Wertsmann, Valdimir Ukrainians in America, Oceana 1976

BIBLIOGRAPHY

Adamic, Louis A Nation of Nations, New York: Harper 1945

American Library Directory New York; R.R. Bowker 1998

Ashton, Rick Genealogy Beginners' Manual, Chicago: Newberry 1977

Bahr, Howard American Ethnicity, Boston: D.C. Heath 1979

Barrett, D. (editor) World Christian Encyclopedia, New York: Oxford University Press 2006

Baxter, Angus Dos and Don'ts for Ancestor Hunters, Baltimore: Genealogical Publishing 1988

Bentley, Elizabeth Genealogist's Address Book, Baltimore: Genealogical Publishing 1998

Drass, G. Ethnic Groups and the State, New York: Barnes & Noble 1985

Brown, Francis and Roucek, Joseph One America, New York: Prentice Hall 1945

Brown, Lawrence Immigration, New York: Macmillan Co, 1936

Cordasso, F. American Ethnic Groups, Bala Cynwyd Pennsylvania: Ayer Press 1981

Danky, James Genealogical Research, Madison Wisconsin: State Historical Society of Wisconsin 1919

Darnay, Brigette and Janice Demaggio Directory of Special Libraries and Information Centers, Detroit: Gale Research 1990

Davie, Maurice World Immigration, New York: Macmillan 1936

Davis, Phillip Immigration and Americanization, Darby, Pennsylvania: Quality Books 1971

DeVos, George Ethnic Identity, Chicago: Univ. of Chicago 1982

Dinnerstein, L. Ethnic Americans, New York; Harper &. Row 1981

Drake, Paul In Search of Family History, Bowie, Maryland: Heritage Books 1992

Duncan, G.H. Immigration and Assimilation, Boston: D.C. Heath 1933

Eakle, Arlene and Johni Cerny The Source, Salt Lake City: Ancestry 1992

Eicholtz, Alice Discovering Your Heritage, Salt Lake City: Ancestry 1992

Filby, William Passenger and Immigration Lists Index, Detroit: Gale Research 1989

Filby,William Directory of American Libraries With Genealogy or Local History Collections, Wilmington: Scholarly 1990

Hess, Fergil High Adventure, San Carlos; Ragusan Press 1970

Handbook of American Orthodoxy, Cincinnati: Forward Pubns. 1972

Hopkins, Garland Your Family Tree, Richmond: Dietz 1949
Kyvig, David Your Family History, Garden City: Harlan 1978

Lankevich, George Ethnic America, Dobbs Ferry, NY: Oceana Publications 1980

Lind, Marilyn Researching Your Family History, Cloquet, Minnesota Linden Tree 1986
Maldando, Lionel Urban Ethnicity in the United States, Beverly Hills: Sage Publications 1985

McCready, William Culture, Ethnicity, and Identity, New York: Academic Press 1982

Meier, Vjakoslav The Slavonic Pioneers of California, San Carlos: Ragusan Press 1968

Rosen, Philip Ethnicity in American Life, Notre Dame Indiana: Notre Dame Press 1979

Smith, Jessie Ethnic Genealogy, Westport Connecticut: Greenwood Press 1983

Sowell, Thomas Ethnic America: A History, New York: Basic Books 1983

Stephenson, George History of American Immigration, Boston: Ginn and Company 1926

Stipanovich, Joseph Slavic Americana, San Carlos: Ragusan 1977

Stratton, Eugene Applied Genealogy, Salt Lake City: Ancestry 1991

Subject Guide to Books in Print, New York: R.R. Bowker 2012

The Official Catholic Directory, New York: P.J. Kenedy 2012

The 1998 IMS-Ayer Directory of Publications, Fort Washington, Pennsylvania: IMS Communications 1998

Turner, Eugene We The People: An Atlas of America's Ethnic Diversity, New York: Scribners 1987

Ulrich's International Periodicals Directory, New York: R.R. Bowker 2011

Ward, David Cities and Immigrants, New York: Oxford University Press 1971

Watkins, M.J. Ancestor Hunting, Baton Rouge, Louisiana: Claitors 1969

Yearbook of American and Canadian Churches, Nashville; Abingdon Press 2012

www.ingramcontent.com/pod-product-compliance
Lightning Source LLC
Chambersburg PA
CBHW070251290326
41930CB00041B/2450